Lightning of Your Eyes

New and Selected Poems

For Pearl, Victor, Kevin, Daniel and Russell.

Lightning of Your Eyes

New and Selected Poems

Chris Searle

Published 2006
by

Smokestack Books
PO Box 408, Middlesbrough TS5 6WA
Tel : 01642 813997
e-mail : info@smokestack-books.co.uk
www.smokestack-books.co.uk

Copyright Chris Searle 2006
All rights reserved

Cover design and print by
James Cianciaruso
j.cianciaruso@ntlworld.com

Cover: Photograph by Arthur Winner
Photograph of Chris Searle
by Sharon Lough

ISBN 0-9551061-1-7

Smokestack Books
gratefully acknowledges the support of
Middlesbrough Borough Council
and Arts Council North East.

Smokestack Books is a member of
Independent Northern Publishers
www.northernpublishers.co.uk

Versions of some of these poems were originally published in *Mainland* (Calder and Boyars, 1974), *Red Earth* (Journeyman Press, 1980) and *Common Ground* (Artery, 1983).

Contents

C.N.R. 9
Soldiers 11
Greyhound 13
Skid Row 14
Boys 15
Flying Over Cuba 16
A Dream of Alfred Linnell 17
Stepney Plane Trees 26
Strike of Words 27
Lil and Bill 28
Poem for Blair Peach 30
To My English Teacher 31
The 17th June Farm 32
Isaac Rosenberg's Earth 33
Des Warren's Eyes 34
Victor Jara 35
Light of Africa 37
Plant the Tree of Freedom Everywhere ! 38
Today's Task is to Pick Cashew 40
Monster 41
Continuadores 43
Those Words 45
A Son's Geography 46
George Lansbury's Dream of Poplar 47
Hawksmoor's Lantern 49
Creation Story 51
Carriacou Lullaby 52
Island Winds 53
Beloved Banditti 57

Maurice and Samora at Seamoon 61
To the Cuban Doctors of Grenada 63
Surprised 65
Workers' Parish Council 66
A Sloop called *Success* 68
Balthazar's Poem 73
What I Have Learned 75
Banner 77
The White Man's Poem to the Black Man 78
Windward Song 80
Burston Fireplace 81
Her First Letter 84
Food of Words 86
To Sylvia Under the Eucalyptus Trees 87
Birdsong 88
Made 90
Poem for Shaif 92
Adjectives 93
My Two Grandmothers 95
As My Mother Knits Blankets for Ethiopia ... 100
No Supertram Over Here ! 103
Third Man 105
Raising a Sightscreen 107
Priceless 108
Ambushed 111
Toronto Transit 114
Passage 116
Hello Siva 118
The Bridge 119

Notes 122

C.N.R.

Ten hours past Toronto,
It seems a dark world is being blown to me,
Primeval forests loom outside
As I drink up with some soldiers,
And at a place called Capreol
I flake out until we reach Winnipeg,
And there we buy a crate of beer.

All senses marvelling across the prairies
As the yellow flatness turns to gold -
When you are young and drunk and crashing through
The new space of the world,
With nothing fixed in your life,
And people are showing you themselves
As if they know that this will be your only meeting,
And you must know all.

And they wish you good luck in this great mass of earth,
And a fat, beaming woman gives you a lucky dollar,
And an old railwayman winks and passes you a cigar,
And a young, pale nun says she will pray for you
That you will soon find work -
And I believe her as I see this generosity,
This mainland all around me.

And talking to the trainman,
Who came from near me in England, a Londoner
Now turned priest of Canada as it whirls past -
And he takes me to the cab and sits me with the driver,
And the fireman shares his coffee
And sweet, ripe peaches from the Okanagan.

I see the sun rising in West Saskatchewan,
And the swamp birds on the line before the engine
Scattering as the train rumbles towards them,
And flapping back to their low lakes.
And I seem to be dividing the world,

Cutting through unfallen hugenesses
Like one of the Earth's inheritors
There, with twenty dollars in my pocket,
As mountains pass, beckoning me with invitations,
And I take in the wild scent of the pines.

In a line drawn across a continent
The great train tears onwards, looking for the sea,
Following a grey, loping river through grim canyons
As it plunges through the mainland,
Carrying me with the mainland.

Canada, 1967

Soldiers

I see them on the buses,
I see them on the trains,
The planes. the roads, in the restaurants -
Soldiers.

Young men, perplexed,
Staring at their own uniforms in bewilderment,
Wondering how they were ever
Soldiers.

Now exposed, the skin on the backs of their necks
Shivers, as they gaze
At the plaques on their breasts which tell them
Their names.

Some, quiet and self-conscious,
Read philosophy through their glasses,
Taking themselves away from the threatening world
Of action.

Talk to them,
They do not try to vindicate themselves,
They only hope their term will be
In Germany or Spain.

Vietnam : the name rings in their ears
Like Death knocking at their suburb,
Making it a place of sudden, violent
Life.

They are not humorous about their chances,
One in ten will go there, they say,
And some of those will
Die.

There is something in their eyes,
which is not doubt,
Because they have no doubts, they are
unwilling.

Their looks are mirrors of defeat,
They move laggingly, like prisoners.
They do not look like
Soldiers.

America, 1968

Greyhound

Beside me, a young Jewish boy
Hung up about his
Puerto Rican girlfriend
Pours out worried confessions.
In front, a white soldier
Tells me about the Cong
Sitting in the trees right above him
Who nearly ripped open his crotch
With their bullets.
Behind me, a black soldier
Smoothes away
With a brown-skinned girl
He has just met
Who smiles as he says, Shit man,
I'm not going out there.
And near Winston-Salem
We blow a tyre
And we all get out
And push together.

North Carolina, 1968

Skid Row

Outside huge towers of light,
Exhausted pits, eyes of darkness stare
And crawl like black crabs over worn faces -
While sprightly people step past,
Wearing badges for their favourites.

Propped by dingy porches,
In their own sanctuaries
They hold fast to grimy bottles,
And esoteric judgements pass from face to face
As the world steps by with its slogans.

'Yeah, when I get me outa here,
I got cousins in Canada -
They got a farm in B.C.
An' I guess I'm headin' there
In a month or two'.

White liquid tilts inside the bottles
And runs fast down stretched throats,
As stomachs heave inwards to themselves,
And collapsing, cover leather belts
When the bare arm falls away.

Unswept sidewalks -
Beds for fallen people,
While men choose presidents
And go for rings
Around the moon.

Chicago, 1968

Boys

While kites eclipse the sun
And fly with the wind,
And boys haul on strings,
Keeping their toes entrenched in the sand,
Men, under roofs of palm branches,
Peruse the sea.

Boys splash in the surf
Crashing their fists against the waves -
Black fishes falling under thrashing gates of water
And coming up shaking,
While men pass nets across their knees
And look for holes.

Boys kick a ball on a hard, damp beach
And shout with screams of joy,
Pass me the ball nah man
Pass me the ball -
While men carry cane on their shoulders
And their cutlasses shine.

Boys on bamboo rafts beyond the surf
Row along the bay,
And their friends turn somersaults through the foam
And swim towards them,
While men in gardens on the cliffside
Dig for yams.

Boys throw wood to the tops of trees,
And with long sticks, poke towards the heart
While green nuts fall like dead men,
And roll and stop in silence -
As men whistle tunes and walk home
From the gardens.

Tobago, 1969

Flying Over Cuba

Down there is Fidel
And the tracks of Che.
And look ! the coastline
Of a map I once knew.

Why do I miss out this island ?
Why is Caribair not Cuban air ?
Why do the flights and fares
Connecting these islands
Exclude that blurring surf below ?

What I will see next
Will not be Cuba,
Jamaica is minutes away,
The Dungle, West Kingston.

The world changes in minutes.

1968

A Dream of Alfred Linnell

For Kevin Gately and Gurdip Singh Chagger

*'Our friend who lies here has had a hard life, and met with a hard death; and if society had been differently constituted, his life might have been a delightful, a beautiful and a happy one. It is our business to begin to organise for the purpose of seeing that such things shall not happen; to try to make this earth a beautiful and happy place.'
(William Morris, speaking at Linnell's funeral)*

As they struck me down, I dreamed a dream.

The hoofs had left me broken and sprawling.
Another lump with the horse droppings in those fine streets
To be shovelled and swept into the gutters of Northumberland

    Avenue

But my comrades picked me up, from under the very heels of death
And carried me away, through streets lined with a hungry throng -
Hungry like I was, and jobless to boot ;
The very reasons for my angry marching,
Through the flying stones and crashing windows
Through the shouts and cries of misused men
They bore me, their bodies wilting with my dying weight,
To a place where suddenly the air was full of calm.

There was dignity and peace, and a great crowd marching,
Marching past Trafalgar Square, where grief-faced men doffed their

    caps at me

As I lay, coffined and covered, lifted by my comrades.
Yet though all who watched saw me confined,
Shut in death's box, another ended man
Who left no wealth for his family, no vacant space at his workplace,
No holy words from his priest, no day's work for a gravestone

    carver -

I found myself huge like mankind, as vast as its history,
And no box could take my limits, no death my new beginning.
Truth to tell, I looked down upon my funeral
And my funeral was the march of the world
With all the men and women who ever worked in my struggling part
                                                  of the city.

For Eastwards it was we marched, Eastwards they carried me
Through that City, that fortress of the moneymaker
Those walls of stone that grew to some men's greed,
Those streets which never opened life to men like me
But only gave me right of way in death.

Past Aldgate where John Ball had stood in all the power of the peasant
And Tyler shouted down the walls that kept them poor,
Through the grimy valleys of Whitechapel where Flemish weavers
Had struggled manfully for Wilkes and liberty
And Mendoza the Jew had boxed to Science and greatness -
Through these streets they bore me, bore me homeward.
And men and women pledged to me, vowing vengeance,
Vowing completion, success, victory and humanity
And I saw and heard it all, watching from my everlastingness,
As over the cobbles we travelled, to Mile End and Bow,
Thousands moving towards my lot of earth.
And people scrambled over mounds, over tombstones,
Between pillars and plinths, columns and angels, marbles and carved
                                                  wood,
Over the bones of seamen and chandlers, lightermen and sailmakers,
Cabinet makers and carpenters, river pilots and garment makers -
They surged around my grave, respectful but angry,
Mourning yet organising, dutiful yet mighty,
Unleashing yet a tiny spark of massiveness
As the rain fell in November, dripping from the London plane trees

That overhung my part of the ground, and bowed their branches
                                                                                             to me.

Headlam read some solemn words over that gone part of me
And Morris' great beard shook the rain from its midst
As he spoke of me with love and brotherliness
And sung out his death song, roaring with his great mane
                                                                                            throbbing
The words of might that stretched through all the power of
                                                                               the language
Towards me, me, a working man appalled at lack of work
And lack of Justice, lack of the organisation men need
To fulfil their lives and love their peers
And set man to man or man to woman or woman to woman
In a life of love and discovery of all the great potential of the
                                                                                                 world
And all its people - me, now all around could not but return
                                                                            that fraternity.
And I was every man and woman that ever thought or sang for
        freedom in those streets,
Or fought for respect and equity mid the canals, the docks,
The terraces, factories, workshops, sweatshops and blocks,
Every man and women who from the tenement of their world
                                                                     lived to make life better.
I was William Blake walking through the chartered riverside
                                                                                   streets
Where houses, masts and heads hung low, waiting for
                                                                           regeneration,
I was Charles Dickens standing under the lantern of
                                                                  Limehouse Church
Making words shine like beacons for the sake of the downtrodden,
I was Jack London from the wharves of San Francisco, the ice
                                                                        of the Klondike

Wilfully scaling down to the human hell of the abyss
And sharing suffering to tell and prove to the world.
I was Thomas More, dreaming man's Utopia at Stepney Green,
John Donne making puns under the growing mulberry trees
Planted by the Hugeonots to feed the silkworms,
I was Ben Jonson laying bricks and forging plays in the new streets
                                    of Spitalfields,
I was Arthur Morrison howling my rage through the dens of the
                                    Jago,
Joseph Conrad, learning my new language through the rigging
                                    of Wapping
And stretching my symbols far beyond the Shadwell Entrance,
I was Gustave Doré drawing on my sheets with the black ink
                                    of indignation,
I was Isaac Rosenberg working my images in a damp, cracking
                                    garret in Stepney,
Forcing my weak chest towards the capitalists' war to pay for
                                    my mother's maintenance
And championing my sensitivity through the tyrants' trenches.
I was Paul Robeson with my notes of kind black thunder shaking
                                    the People's Palace.
Mahatma Gandhi living, breathing, learning, taking struggle from
                                    the people of Bow,
I was Christopher Caudwell, writing, analysing, fighting, organising,
Leaving all behind to serve his brothers in the dry rocks of Castile,
I was all those certainly, and I was more.

I was every gasworker that ever stoked a stinging fire in Beckton
And stood by the retort's shaking flames, taking brute heat -
I was with Will Thorne when we took our eight hour day.
I was every dockworker whoever pulled a pulley in Millwall,
                                      stood in the cage,
Was left on the stones or lay with his limbs crushed at Blackwall
                                      Yard.

I was with Ben Tillett when he spoke like fire through his
                              stammer to us at the gates,
Swinging his spiked mace into a wealth of stevedores and
                              dockers
As he goaded our resistance in the morning mists rising from the
                              Isle of Dogs.
With Harry Orbell when we pushed back a trainload of
                              blacklegs
With our bare strengths, organised together.
I was Tom Mann, leading thousands singing down the
                              Commercial Road,
Riding with ships upon wheels, brandishing our stingy sausage
                              meals at our employers,
Clamouring for more justice and more money
Flexing the muscles of a new class in history.
I stood with the matchgirls at Bow, scratching my jaw for the
                              curse of the phosphorus,
Pelted with mildewed fruit the statue of Gladstone,
                              erected from our wages.
Cutting our wrists as our women's blood ran down its length.
I was William Morris, spreading out my poems from the corner
                              of Dod Street,
Holding off the batons of policemen who tore at our banners,
And yes, I was Alfred Linnell, crushed by the ordered horses
                              of the State,
An exile from Bow killed in the fairways of power.
I was Sylvia, writing late into the night at Old Ford
For the next day's Dreadnought, and the next week's struggle
                              and arrest,
Force-fed and beaten inside the dull bricks of Holloway,
Shouting down the imperialist war in the market places of
                              Poplar,
Inspiring all our women to stand up, stand up for their lives

And take all their joys and money-held, man-held freedoms.
I was with the East India dockers when we shunned the Jolly George.
Not loading or fuelling a ram against the workers
Whether in Russia, Cuba, China or Chile.

I set up speaking platforms in the street for Harry Pollitt,
Marched with George Lansbury to Brixton Prison
And walked back to Poplar after his words split the prison bars.
I shared the dying moments of Minnie Lansbury as she too pushed
                                            aside the zooming rate,
The cold, growing burden of her neighbours,
Stood with Nellie Cressall in her labour pains at Holloway,
Took on the troops as we held fast in 1926,
Cursed with my mates at the betrayals of our leaders
And the armed phalanx of soldiers who guarded the blacklegs.
I whooped with joy as the fascists ran from us in Cable Street
And stood arm in arm with Jew and black man at the barricades.
I looked up with my people towards the blitz of Nazi bombs,
And with the world, fought back the night that came in daytime,
Taking our lives and hopes and hard-won freedoms.

All these lives I shared as the rain fell, and the wet earth slithered
                                                          over me,
Scraping the wood that covered my bruised flesh -
Then all the people vanished from my sight, all buildings,
                                                        brick and smoke.
Only the river, deep and dark, tidal with the moon, stayed with me,
Mud and stones exposed from its raw banks.
Marsh, swamp and limepit, overhanging reeds,
Empty of the light of people.

Then Eastwards from a roman city crept out the wood and brick,
Saxon farm and meadow combed from the matted grassland,
And the long ships of the Norsemen edged along the banks

And miscegenation thrived, all along the river.

From the Sussex coast moved up the Norman swords,
Making laws, seeking consensus, speaking new words.
Power grew with the barons, blessed by the Church,
But peasant blood raged with the sweeping river.

Then craft built our suburbs - persecuted from France
The 'Fourniers', 'Fleurs-dy-lys', 'Nantes' of the Huguenots
Crossed shores and made cloth, wove skills with the Flemish,
Making first stitches in the garments of our greatness.

East India, West India - Empire made slaves of the world,
And rich men ordered docks, berths for their treasures.
So, leaving their strips of land, their herd of goat or cow,
The people came, changing earth for dust and stone.
Men from the western sea, speaking in new rolling accents
Walked new streets with a shovel and a pick.
And out of the marsh came solidness, hardness -
Quayside rose from mud and meadowland, as Irish breath
                                  made new lines of progress.

And the ships brought sugar, shares and profit,
Not made by the sailors who had boarded them at the Gold Coast,
Not made by the blackened men who scooped the coal from their
                                  planks,
Not made by the ironsmiths who built the Great Eastern and
                                  steamed our country forward.

For whom ? For whom ?
Not to the Jews to whom our river made life's arteries flow again,
As pogroms crushed their hopes and breaths and futures
And our narrow streets blazed wide for their struggles.

But for a new class of barons - in that City, that granite burden of
                                              the working people
Which prospered on their pain and labour,
Pleasured on the toil of all their hands and brains,
Looked to crush a world-wide class with its craft and cunning.

From the islands in the necklaced sea came people,
Their history grounded in sugar and the bitter taste of the slave.
Boats sailed northward, bound with hopes and myths,
To drive and oil the new machines and onward transport
                                              of the world.
Those came from the west -
And from the east, to find fulfilment, find the centre,
Came brown-skinned people, eager to work and organise,
Reaching a strange, wished-for land with hostile mouths and insults
                                              scrawled on walls.
Here they came, and as with the others,
They stayed and worked and mixed, and built and learned
                                              and struggled -
As we all have, as we all do - all have, all do,
To make these streets softened with the flesh of living people,
To make these walls invisible for the crossing smiles of men and
                                              women,
To make these houses filled with the hopeful laughs of children,
To make these estates shine with all the colours of the human,
To make this river run free with the will of structured love.
From those who came, to those who come,
Sprung from the multitudes stems the one.
Out of the rubble
Beyond the storm
Rooted in history
A new world is born.

The earth yawned above me : rain and soil still clattered on my box,
Beneath the rare trees of Bow, Morris still roared his song
                                                    for socialism.
I was beneath and above, past and hence,
Death was but a phase, life began for others -
I saw and heard it, lived it and repeated it.

This dream I dreamed, as they struck me down.

August 6, 1976

Stepney Plane Trees

What nurtured you ?
Some people say
The air which makes you beautiful
Is killing the world.

Your leaves are girls' faces
Your leaves soften London.
Your mottled trunk, peeling face
Tells of your stoicism.
Your itchy-backs make me laugh
Hanging like ear-rings,
And when they fall
Singing children kick them down the road.

How can you grow in this air ?
How can you flourish while
Rushing artics, roaring engines
Give you your breath ?

A city's beauty is a brave beauty.

1971

Strike of Words

Anyone can write a poem, I still hold that,
But you children, sharply organised,
You made your words strike,
The words of your class march
Past middle-class poet-cynics
Shaking their heads, declaring
'Poetry can do nothing,
It makes nothing happen.'

Yes, *their* poetry can do nothing
morosely making nothing of the world,
But yours, wed to action
Can take it over.

Priests who lived for learning shackles
And dullards hanging onto power
Saw their enemies in you, in us,
And with your shouting, loyal words
You blew them over with your poetry.
All down Stepney Green their bars are broken,
Along Commercial Road the poisoned air clears.
In Stepney Churchyard the grass shines in pride.

Children of word and fire
Yellowbrick children of docks and tenement
You made me what I am,
Your words carved me out a new mind -
I work to make myself
Worth the winning.

Stepney, 28 March 1971

Lil and Bill

Early in the Stepney morning
as I walked to school
    up Bromley Street
your door would open for me

Lil you'd just finished
    cleaning the classrooms
and Bill stood by the front door
the tenth door up the long terrace
he waved his stick at me
come and have a cup of tea son

He told me about navy days
days of U boats, days of war
days of struggle
he poured drops of whiskey in my tea
they bobbled up and winked at me
and sent me on my way to school

And on a Spring day in May
when the children chalked my name
    on the school walls
and told the guvnors not to sack me
Lil, they ordered you to rub it off
they told all the cleaners
    to rub off the words

You all said no
you were with the children
as they sang outside the school
as they marched through the banks of the City
as they waved their banners
    along the Embankment
    next to the swilling Thames they laughed

as they dipped their toes in the fountains
as they climbed the lions
    in Trafalgar Square
you were with the words
you shared the poems
you were with me

How can I forget you
    now old myself
your whiskey drops still boil in my blood
your mop still cleans my mind
every morning
as I remember my way to school

Poem for Blair Peach

His was a precious, loving life..
He built his passion with great bridges
   from the farthest islands of the southern seas
    to the mist that clears in the classrooms of Bow -
Life was too short to stand injustice.
   to stand the insults that he saw around him :
Humans used as pawns
Humans named as the blame for sorrow
   that they themselves felt and lived !
He saw and lived oppression on his pulses -
Colours to him were beauty,
   not a form of self-made blindness !
The human is a beaming jewel,
   from New Zealand to the streets of Southall
   he shone with its brilliance !

You who seek to murder beauty - understand !
It rises with the dawn of every day
It stays and glows with the moon and the stars
It screams with the lungs of every new-born child
It reasons with the truth of every thinking human -
Never forget the blood that crosses oceans,
Blair's brave heart swells to fill us all.

To My English Teacher

To Norman Hidden

Sitting in a classroom once, you showed me poetry.
I was young and full with cricket on my cheeks
And words seemed only messages of action
Swapped by normal people, living in unquestioned ways.

Now I think I know how hard it must have been
To make words laugh and cry and feel.
For they can cross well-ordered avenues, melt the
    suburbs of the brain
And reach that part within that reaches out.

It is, and seems like, years ago
That those poems prised away the boulders heaped upon me.
Stone upon stone they lifted off -
You were the worker with the lever.

There is a language that people speak
And that same language makes poetry.
But how to make words walk naked
Yet clothed in all the love and progress of the human ?

That's the contradiction that we seek to heal,
The tension that I learned through your direction.
For words are solid, they can build creations
That make men's hopes take form and life and permanence.

The 17th June Farm

The bark stops suddenly, halfway down the trunks
Like rolled-up trouser bottoms
In the cork orchards of Alentejo.
The legs of the trees are firm and tanned,
And the peasants now own the horizon-full land.

For here the people have roots in their earth
Freshly planted by new determination,
Confirmed and won by June's expropriation -
Love and labour swelled until it found
The victory of the earth and man.

A harvest doubled since the land was theirs,
Their landlord in Brazil, crushed by his fears,
His priests gone crawling back to God, his deceiving
 turned to tears.
His church now a granary to store through their years
The reaping of hard-won ideas
That gave them land, and will and wheat.

Even the bull proudly snorts his freedom
And rolls his head with new abandon.
No longer the fascist bull whose horns gored breath
From faces now shining with pride and welcome.
And children roll in the grass, their future springs
 with the cork trees.
And smiles and eyes reflect the sun of all their possibilities.

Alcaçer do Sal, Portugal. December 1975

Isaac Rosenberg's Earth

Remote from Stepney streets, you lie in French earth.
Your brothers are around you, all sides are full of men -
All the earth of foot-treads, end to end the tyrants' saving.
Some they called your friends, some they called your
   enemies,
But all were the fount of your song
Of words and beauty, love-blasted from your heart.

Genius burst from you with the strength of flowers,
And trees that smoke and brick ground to the roots -
How they conspired to contain you, to patronise you !
You died, making words for all our meaning, trampled to the mud.
But the earth and you thrive under concrete, under tar
For your children of poetry, walking these streets.

Des Warren's Eyes

Des
    You're a brave man -
I know you well
I've met you in every glowing eye
of a man and woman
        knowing and feeling

                deciding

they are trying to change the world
they are going to change the world.

Every determined voice that shouts
        'Yes,
we shall struggle !'
is your voice, plain and strong
clear
like gushes of water
springing from the ground
and rushing, gathering
        inseparable

           one force
to take its will to the world
and carve its shape
        mould it
            transform it.

Thus, those shining drops
        flash in your eyes
reflect ours
make our shared, pounding force.
Des
    You're a brave man -
I know you well
when I look at my brothers' eyes
        my sisters' eyes
your eyes.

Victor Jara

How can a name
>cut
>sharp as love

through the cruelty of the darkness
from the other side of the world
>>where men parade

as fleshless, morbid fiends ?
Victor
>your sounds, your words say
>>'Man is a maker'

a maker of words
>a maker of actions
>>of earth-sweeping revolutions

of love,
>sharp, cutting love.

Can gun-butts crush such force
Which rises up from your peasant earth
>>through Neruda's great forests

to find the consciousness of every working human
who stops his toil to listen ?
Do you know what makes you live
In the warm breast of the flesh of the world ?
Do you know what makes you strum and sing
In the heads of men and women willed with change ?
Your every deathless cell
>your blood
>>they caused to flow

from the tools of your beauty,
>is the plectrum
>>clear and cutting

pricking the rising tide of love inside us
making a flood
>of living blood

not to be spilled on the fascist's captured earth
wired inside his crippling compounds,
but to flow like Amazons
               through the myriad veins
of love's new irrigation
               of her People's rising victories
of the new world !

Light of Africa

In the shimmering light of mid-day
And the lightest nights I have known,
When the moon defines the world
With a glowing tint of recognition,
Making the darkness visible and clear -
I remember my childhood
And the fear of dark continents.

There, in the bowels of ignorant schools
They told us of darkness here, only darkness,
Of savagery and blood, of black men in trees,
Of the white man's beacon and the Bible's light,
Of the flag and Empire and redcoated hero,
Of the man with the moustache who was carried through swamps,
Who marvelled at the cascading waters he discovered
(The customary sight of those who carried him),
And the foreign handshake which switched on the light -
This was Civilisation, we presumed.
From the Cape to Cairo, this was our ground.
The red ink in our atlases convinced us
Our stamp collections told us it was true !

The darkness of those who came !
The blind eyes of their settling offspring
The obscurantism of the gods of the north
And those who wrote our History books !
Did they never try to look at this brilliant sun
This truth that hurts the eyes
Which penetrates all at its zenith
And leaves no shadows, making us re-learn the world ?

Africa of Samora, of Neto and Cabral !
Sun of Africa, the furnace of your History,
Burn through the lies that cloud our northern skies,
They are grey and dark and need your light.

Plant the Tree of Freedom Everywhere!

In the digging of holes
In making a harvest of compost
In the planting of a tree -
Transforming Nature,
The human is transformed !

The spade in the earth
Meets the pen on the paper,
The swinging curve of the pick
Meets the words on the page.
Doing this, comrades,
We are building the New School !

Through the windows of our classrooms
We see the young orange trees.
These trees that will grow
With the force of our growing bodies
Are our trees !
The tree of slaves is uprooted,
These new roots grip the fertile soil,
The soil is watered by the struggle of Africa
Of parents and grandparents, generations of blood.

Our school and our trees, they grow together.
The brick, the sap, the ideas make the same surge upwards.
Our brains, our flesh, our souls are inside them !
The lives of our children
The juice of their future
The fruit of our conscious work.

Everywhere comrades !
Everywhere, in every place,
In city and village, by concrete and mud,
In every spot of the waiting earth,
Everywhere where the human carries his tools

Loves her people
Covers his head
And lives her life -
Everywhere
Plant the tree of Freedom !

Today's Task is to Pick Cashew

The country brims with the scent of cashew,
The full, red fruits dangle from the trees
The nuts swing beneath them,
They are ready for us.
The sun already scorches the earth
As we wake, overflowing with our task.
We pile onto the backs of a convoy of lorries,
We stand in one mass of flesh,
Our arms are linked, our shoulders are firm together
As we leave the city, the hard cement.
The tyres jump and bounce
And the wheels roll and sink through the sand.
We sing and cry out our songs
We call over the land
Through the round, granite hills
Pointing upwards like blunt fingers -
Our words speak of our comrades in Zimbabwe, in Soweto,
Birds sit on the branches of the cashew trees,
Their red beaks are open
They return our song with a flying joy.
The country joins our chorus,
Women and children on the sides of the road
Show us their raised fists and their radiant smiles
As our lorries roar past them.
Peasants raise their bodies from the earth,
They lift and shake their hoes towards us.
The sky is our endless roof,
The sun has risen on our future
Its brightness is infinite -
All this youth, this huge energy of man and nature,
As we accomplish our words of order :
'Let us all pick cashew !
It is a base of our economy !'

Monster

I saw it today
it was squatting
        poised
couched for the fray,
in a government office.
It perched on the desk
arrogant and sure
like an instrument of torture
  waits for the poor.

Its head was rutted
  with trenches
       palisades
teeth to gnaw
     grind
  and dig like spades
into people
  people
 revolutionary flesh
in this scorching hour
workers and peasants taking power !
One by one they came
queuing for its favours
     for hours
     and hours
to pass by its lair
and bow to its strength
    - it is making war !
The man who turned its wheel
seemed to serve it
 like a fearful retainer
too frightened to feel !

It wasn't like a machine
which a worker operates
it was like a creation
    which malignant, castrates.
It crushes the man who makes it
beats down his mind
    becomes his master
        makes him crawl behind.
Workers beware
like a fixed-eyed snake
    it is watching you
    for your first mistake !
Your enemies are hovering
wherever it goes,
in its head
  are your mortal foes -
crushing your flesh
  the exploiter's charm
twisting its wheel
 the reactionary's arm
Tedium
passivity
and delay
the watchwords
    of the bureaucrat's day -
Swear you will never
    turn into its prey !

Continuadores

Such children
shoeless
singing
striding like heroes
through their conquered city.
A legion of now
      and of the future
the colours of their banner
streak the sky with victory.

Singing songs of revolution
the new combatants
   the conquerors
 the *continuadores*
they surge with the certainty of
life emerging
hope emerging
justice emerging
in every massive, muscled step.

Bare feet like Nature's boots
clumping on the pavement
with their hardened soles,
already
they know the tar
the texture of the earth
the soil of their future
deep
   rich
 fertile with fulfilment -
their flesh is pounding !
And the air they are breathing
is sucked in
   like freedom !

Their unbroken voices
cry out an oratorio
of rising power
    of youth -
smiles which cut the sunlight
ragged
       shoeless
       but triumphant !
They trail onwards together
they wind, endless
to make their own destiny,
singing out their Party's name
in one, united force
to write their own history,
to build a better world.

Those Words

To hear those words
those words of glorious red
 of the world's new sunrise
A LUTA CONTINUA !
echoes through my every cell
    and deepens my blood
makes me surge with hope for the world.
It is your slogan
        here, now,
but you have made it
the slogan
  of every struggling man and woman
every human ground down
with the load of a wretched life
    an exploited life
    an alienated life
a lifetime of oppression.
Those words
they spark every heart
    words of fire
        words of lightning
words of life in formation
words of becoming
  words of flesh and earth
 of tool and concrete
real words.

A Son's Geography

For Victor

You were made in the sun
On the revolutionary earth of Africa.
You were born in a blizzard
Blowing over the roofs of Mile End.
Your mother crossed the Atlantic
For the misty brick of London -
A little girl in ribbons, clasped to her mother
Leaving the blue glow of the Caribbean
And the beach of Carriacou where sun fused with sand
And her grandfather built the strutted skeletons of boats.
Somewhere inside you a Frenchman walks -
You're a human of the world.

You had a great-grandfather who made toys
In the valleys of Abergavenny,
Another was a gamekeeper
Who married a squire's daughter in East Anglia.
He was expelled from the estate
She was disinherited -
They love again inside you.

An Irish midwife opened up the road for you
And you came splashing out.
You were cared for by nurses
From the wards of all the world -
From Hong Kong and India, from Jamaica and Zimbabwe.
The next to take your birth-bed
Was a woman from Bangladesh -
This is the geography of your being
From the map of the world's people,
The history of your flesh
From the blood and bones of others -
You're a human of the world.

George Lansbury's Dream of Poplar

In our beloved triangle
Midst cut and dock and Lea,
I dreamed a future happiness
Of the people strong and free.

There's not much grass in Poplar,
The soil is pressed by stone,
But earth made rich by the flowing Thames
Has a wilful people grown.

Our riches are our people
The jewels are in their eyes,
Their hands have built a city
And their work made a future rise.

The times we marched together,
Striking evil at its root !
We sang, spoke and persuaded,
Seized power from the brute.

The people of the spreading world
Share our doorsteps now,
Our massive strength must forge a life -
One blood, one love to sow.

To own those things we always made,
To organise our power,
To plant new work in dying docks,
Strike the workers' eternal hour !

Fifty years after, I still dream on
And the mist clears over the Thames.
The vision still embraces my heart
And sends the past in flames.

In our beloved triangle
Midst cut and docks and Lea
I dreamed a future happiness
Of the people strong and free.

Hawksmoor's Lantern

From my classroom window I see the stone,
a lantern of stone built on a tower.
It stretches from the traffic
above the fume-stained plane trees,
above the exhaust of desperate engines,
above the confusion
of disordered sounds.
Like a future for us all
it is solid
 symmetrical
    exemplary.
My eyes wander to it daily
from the children's faces
sitting above me.
It has its own face
that stares over Limehouse
 over Poplar
beckons up river
        and does not wrinkle -
I marvel every day
at the sensitivity of this stone,
how can it so speak to me ?

Humans die in our streets
on my days of staring at this stone.
Our people's lives are cut to pieces
and the fragments
drain their splintering bottles
on the benches
    or sprawled across gravestones
below the lantern.
A foreign man is kicked to death
as he exits a train
that has surfaced from the earth.
A brother teacher is clubbed to death
because he sees the colours of life

as a rainbow living
   in the streets of his world.
So one day
   we left our classroom
and upwards we wound
      together we climbed
into the head of this stone
into the mind of this lantern,
   and looked out
filling its spaces with our eyes.
We looked out over our world
   our portion of the earth,
not as an invented god
      glares with fears,
not only as an architect surveys and projects
or an artist makes shapes -
but as people, humans
intent to live and work
   produce and love
change and transform
from our myriad parts of flesh
   still growing,
to the earth and blood of the years to come.
So under the swooping plane trees
in Limehouse Churchyard,
let's have no elegies
no valedictions !
Let's praise human beings and their works and monuments !
Let's praise towers, trees, grass and children !
Let's marvel at the sparking of the future !
Let's vindicate the living, and those yet to live !
For all they know have been gifts
from the dead,
      and so the dead still tower in the sky,
thrust root and live inside us.

Creation Story

Offshore
      from the depths blue as heaven
the volcano rumbles
  under the sea,
submerged
      like the reticence
of the power of the people.
The sea boils like broth
  as the gas spews the waters,
the waves surge outward
  and the island folds
crests sublimely
with the awesome energy of rock and earth
and in its youth and daring
climbs on the back of the sea.

From its sleep
the island wakes,
the muscles stretch
    tightening the dreams of the people
taut, like reality :
'Organisation, our only weapon !' -
    thus shouts the human.
The peasant past is thrown awry
individualism trembles
  in the storm of combination :
the rushing wind
of a red flag unfurled,
changing an island
      into a world.

Carriacou Lullaby

For Kevin

The waves are whispering in your ears,
'Sleep, little brother of the earth,
My sound will wash away your fears
And sweep them through my tender surf.'

Every thrust upon the sand
Of the water's softening breast,
Is your mother's loving hand
A stroke of mighty tenderness.

The rippling waves that form your sheet,
The gleaming sea's eternal sighs,
Will make your sun-filled slumber sweet
And cover the lightning of your eyes.

Your sleeping head against my chest
And all the world's strong future here,
My browning child take all your rest
With water clear as wakefulness.

Through the water's ageless swish,
In the rocking of the sea,
Is the human's heaving wish
That the whole world shall be free.

Island Winds

To the memory of Fitzroy 'Mashie' Williams

Always the wind
sweeping the villages
rattling the pods of pigeon peas
sending the rasp of the donkeys' brays far across the pastures
bending the coconut trees
   bedraggling their leaves
like tattered kites
ginning the lint like an old man's hair
from the unkempt heads of cotton.
Little island
the wind blesses you
with its eternal movement
  its ructions
and its gentleness
its balm
and potent terror.
It blows and wants
to bring new life, new production
to the villages blasted by migration :
Six Roads, Belle Vue
Dumfries and Belmont -
eroded land
    sucked away by you, wind
to Brooklyn, Aruba,
Trinidad, Huddersfield
Shepherd's Bush and Toronto,
the scattered earth of Carriacou
the diaspora of our dust of flesh
    despot wind !

In Belmont the air is fast with breezes
passing over the servant waves
    to the looming edge of your sister
Grenada,

      that roll through the mists
like the backs of giant horses
      springing from the sea
and defining the horizon.
Along the kerbstones the people have painted :
'On our knees never !'
'Free at last !'
'We rather die than to become
  puppets of Imperialism !'
And on a boarded-up shop are new advertisements :
'Stay up Grenada !
We are a big Revolution
in a small country !'
To these words, wind
you bring your freshness
you blow away the dust.
To these rough-painted words
  you breathe a constant life
as the children sing their way to school
along the road to Harvey Vale.

This world to which your people spread
      little island,
counts you but a speck
a piece of dried earth in the sea
a place from which to pluck its strength of arms
and then spit them back with the wind
      when the biceps grow meagre
and their use is over :
the Caribbean is more salty
with their sweat,
 the water more blue
with the history of their bruises.

On March the thirteenth
 when revolution is celebrated
and the militia marches proudly
        along Hillsborough's single street,
and the sea applauds
    with its lapping clapping waves
and along the beachside,
the people shout for Tamayo
the first black man
to climb into space
        and touch the limits of the human's knowledge
with his white comrade.
And here he comes,
resplendent soldier of the future
a Toussaint of the skies
the people heave their faces upwards
the guns of the militia wave in the wind
above the heads of young soldiers,
        men and women
in their home-made uniforms.
The pride is concrete :
    you can build from it
little island,
        you too can sweep the stars
like Tamayo,
and sow your earth with as many seeds.
As the Big Drum pounds
 and the skirts of the dancers
billow in its caresses,
the wind enfolds the beat
 and through the breasted hills of Ma Chapelle
over the Atlantic seas it blasts out
    home to Guinea, home to Benin
to the earth of Ibo and Cromanti

and westwards too
 to new volcanic islands
to the craters of Nicaragua
 across oceans in its orbits
 through the minds of humanity
back to Africa
back to the world
back to the future !

So little island
      I bring you
a foreigner's love
      a stranger's solidarity
but none the less for that.
For the setting free of islands
in the grasp of the earth
in the making of revolution
 that springs from love
all our foreignness is ended.

Beloved Banditti

Monuments to colonialism
 are scattered through the islands
like a pox.
This pink church tower is one of them
although it has its uses
and holds a clock
which measures the hours of the workers of St George's.
It has ticked through two centuries
 and men's struggles
have moved to its chimes.
The colonialists had not only pen and paper
 to propagandise :
they used brick and stone
and carved their lies on marble.
Those who held the power held the pen
And made the mark permanent
 petrified
in this church.
And to pass on the words
like serpentine chasms in this dull-shining brick,
they built their font in front of them
to baptise below their message
and ingrain in the souls of infants
 those words
that currency of power
 which liquidates the lips of humans.

And I too was christened in this church -
next to an Essex farmyard
 an ocean away
but this same loving church
 in a little English village.
And on its walls
 the squires celebrated themselves

and sculpted angels over their bones
and locked their names in history
while the labourers pressed down on their ploughs through the
    thickening clay
or sweated with the great bales of hay
and in the icy dawns of Winter
shivered and squelched with sodden, leaky boots through the
    trespassing dew
with rasping lungs
 and died young,
and over their earthen graves
        were raised no stones, inscribed no words :
only a wooden cross which crucified their lives.

So where are the words which put value on the workers ?
Where are the sentences which celebrate the rebels ?

The Revolution must carve them
        in greater elements than stone -
Where is the monument
to remember the warriors ?
The Revolution must build it
in the heads of the workers
in the minds of the peasants
in the brains of the fishermen
in the knowledge of the teachers.

For after Fedon's flaming years
and after the red of fire and Revolution
had striped Grenada's green with blood and freedom,
the colonialists massacred
those who had lifted their heads towards the sun
and with *the blessings*
   of the British Constitution

they took the hero Chasteau,
Fedon's first lieutenant
(for Fedon had flown the way of freedom)
and they locked him in a cage

    suspended him over Point St Eloi
and starved him to death

  (having already tortured
and quartered
and removed the intestines
and burned alive
several of his comrades).
Then they went to this church
and carved this stone

    thus
compleating the measure of their iniquity
and preaching,

    as they were great preachers
of *diabolical and unprovok'd cruelty* -
then they prayed
and baptised their children
and sat in the front pews
and leaving their whips with their overseers
next Sunday they prayed again
and still they pray !

But those *execrable banditti*
  accursed freedom-mongers !
Let us blow their names, their words like conches
across the golden strands of the Caribbean

    and over the world -
for rebellion was their baptism
and they were born again
 every day
in smoke and blood.

For Fedon christened Butler, christened Maurice
and blew his song to love and liberty
to black man
     white man
brown man -
to Bogle, to Bolivar
to Marti, to Marx
to Zapata, to Connolly
to Garvey, to Gramsci
to Lenin, to Sandino
to Che, to Cabral
to Angela, to Ho Chi Minh
to Fidel, to Samora -
these comrades of life
humans of hope
makers of certainty
we march with you
beloved banditti !

Maurice and Samora at Seamoon

Through a gap in the coconut trees
I saw the waves
 rearing up
and bursting in their frenzy
as if they too
 were straining to see
to tell their brothers and sisters
rising
      swelling
         pounding
across the world
the truth of what we saw
the force of what we saw -
Maurice and Samora at Seamoon.

The same waves
 the same sea
the bitter waves
 the bitter sea
waves of waywardness
sea of separation
human torn from human
earth ripped from earth
and all cry out
from shore to shore
'Four hundred years,
   we shall take no more !'

History heals its wounds
through the nurse of struggle,
the flesh joins up
 across the cuts

and is harder, more knowing
for the new flesh
    is revolutionary flesh
and it forms
    triumphantly
never to sunder
    as we stand in wonder
as Samora shouts
    'A luta continua !'
As Maurice shouts
    'Forward Ever !'
Maurice and Samora at Seamoon.

At Seamoon
    the world is Africa,
the fresh rain is the blood of Africa
it falls upon us all,
the spilling sun is the sun of Africa
it shines upon us all,
Grenada is Africa
the little children are Africa
I, the white man, am Africa.
For when Samora sings
  'Kannimambo Grenada !'
as the band roars out with
    'Forward March !'
this clasp of hands
    has made one world
one Africa
    one future for the human -
Maurice and Samora at Seamoon !

To the Cuban Doctors of Grenada

You know about heartbeats
you know the throb of the world
and the profound pulse of its children.
Your own hearts pump love and renewal,
they fill the cisterns of a new life.

To live with money, yes -
that is everybody's burden.
But not to live for it !
To live for life
and to make life healthier,
to organise the body of the human
all humans
the man digging cassava in Angola
the woman picking peas in Carriacou
the child tending goats in Iraq
the youth teaching letters in Nicaragua.

I see you with the people
  in their houses,
on their boats, their roads -
    no gulf between you
no chasms of professional preening !
Organs of the people,
their sentinels, their embrocation
talking, advising
    joking, soothing
your home their place of consultation
your foreign voice their code of remedy.

As I give you English lessons
I learn your thirst to learn.

One day you wrote for me :
'To be an internationalist
  is to pay a debt
to humanity'.
You asked me, 'Is that correct ?'
What could I say ?
What did I say ?
'Yes brother, that is correct.'
You flow in life's artery
and your island floats with you
    in curing waters
to any land of humans,
 in the course of Che
in the veins of Fanon and Bethune
in the bright eyes of Cheddi
in the blood of Agostinho.
I met you in Africa
    I meet you in Grenada :
You work to heal the world.

Surprised

As I pass on a bus
Words on a wall
   marching
across a ruined house :

As you wake, cry unity !
They startled my brain
               my eyes trembled
the imagination burst
squeezed in my seat
        I knew I must
blaze them across my heart.

Brain
   eyes
      imagination
         heart
waking like never before
working like never before
revolutionary senses
            touched
and sprung.

Workers' Parish Council
To Selwyn Strachan and Martin Carter

Comrade, it is yours
the microphone is yours
it is a machine of life
  grasp it
and speak to its head
your voice belongs inside it
    and through it
passing to the people
the words of recognition
words like arms to hold your comrades close
to criticise
    to reprove
        to suggest
   to educate
grasp it
it is part of your voice
  your will.
Let it carry your formulation
for you are the architect,
let it carry bricks
for you are the builder,
let it carry you home
for these are the words you must live with
they build the house of your democracy
grasp it
      it is yours !
Old woman cracking nutmegs, grasp it !
Young man of the co-operative, grasp it !
Woman driving the tractor, grasp it !
Student with books and fork, grasp it !
Revolutionary soldier, grasp it !
Farmer with hands gnarled like the tannia skin, grasp it !

It will explain you
      connect you
  teach you
    free you
grasp it !
    Yours !

A Sloop called *Success*

The waves pound the planks
and creak the curling keel,
and I hold my pen helplessly
in the welter of waters.
The sloop *Success* is dancing
rocking on the wave tips,
balanced between the sweeping clouds
sped by the wind
with the swiftness of seagulls,
and the awesome sea
which, so turbulent in its mindlessness
gives my pen little chance.
But I jab and stab
and scrape down words
hugging the stern like a squid,
and the *Success* sails on,
a cell of moving humans
stacked up with fruit and letters
bananas and callaloo
yam, dasheen and sweet potato
tossed in sublimity
across a crushing sea.
Ideas strike me like the spray
soaking me piece by piece,
and my mind rolls like the waves
as the words struggle to leave it
like the flying fishes
break like spears from the sea
and for priceless gleaming seconds
we behold their darting shape.

Comrade Poets, we are not things of beauty,
if we are to be anything

we are to be
beings of usefulness !
If we are to live like humans
what we must make
are words to change the world -
for nothing else was language conceived
and for nothing else
will a human poet use it !
Our poetry must fight
to void the void
get out of the self
of the one man's secret mind-jail
untangle our words
get out of the wood
first and foremost
be understood !

We legislate nothing !
We do not make laws
we cannot be arrogant.
To make laws and structures
is the task of the collective
who work the earth
and give us our riches
We serve humanity, yes
that is clear as words.
We rebel as humanity
our solidarity is with its vision,
with its freedom
with its justice
with its exploited who will be rich in the earth
with its wretched who will share a new birth
with its poor who will truly know their worth

and its children
its bursting youth
whose muscles of freedom
will cause the end of hatred
and make the masonry
of the structures of love.

As I write this poem
I cross the length of water
between two revolutionary islands
in this small bouncing boat
carrying the mail
messages of love and work
words in the wind
rocking with the white horses
and the moving cordilleras
and the restless, straining spirit
of the endless sea.
Beneath us hisses
the hidden, mountain cone
of a submarine volcano -
sharing its exuberance
the ancestors named it 'Kick 'em Jenny'.
It boils up the sea
which sits on its heat
and steams with its power
like all the words inside us,
all those said and those unsaid,
promised
yet to be conceived -
the words boil up within us,
the future's volcano

goads up its pressure
rousing a sea of humans
to the truth of Revolution.
A crewman passes me
a swig of scorching rum
it burns my vitals
like the irrepressible lava
of all-consuming change !
As the bow leaps
to the foam and the splattering spray
and the agonised sails
blowing inwards to their limits
struggling with the tearing wind
carry us forward, a community
of us, the humans
moving through our world,
with the volcanic might below us
erupting in our every move to freedom :

the sailor with his wire trawling for barracuda
the rastaman with his hat with the colours of Africa
the old woman coming home from her daughter in the sister island
the Indian man with his bananas to sell in Monday's market
the revolutionary soldier with a badge of Che on his beret
the little girl cured of sickness going back to her parents
the returned immigrant telling me of my streets in London
the people, the makers of language
the judges of poetry -
and I, the teacher,
travelling from task to task
grasping time to make a poem
writing lines in the stern

watching the swirling wake
foaming, the mad mouths of the sea
wild, like the fire in my head
my words only commentary
on the spilling energy
the human changing nature
and with his working craft
cutting through the waters
changing himself, herself
like every curling wave,
unique and relentless
in this wild and smothering sea.

And with this language
we shall blow, we shall flame
and with the force of volcanoes
the wind and the sea
like this little sloop
this little *Success*
full to the brim with hope, fruit and humans
we shall come to harbour.

Balthazar's Poem

I was born a white boy
  in a white man's world.
I never met a black man
  except Man Friday
  and whispers of the Mau-Mau.
When I was ten in the London suburbs
they covered me with black boot polish
all over arms, face, legs
  put a crown on my head
and I was the King of Ethiopia,
Balthazar they called me
    bringing myrrh to Jesus -
whatever that was, they never told me.
It took a month to rub the blackness off
and I was chapped and red and raw like pigmeat.

The first black man I ever met
was a man called Wesley Hall.
I was thirteen
    he was an unknown sportsman
on his first tour of my country.
I asked for his autograph at Ilford Cricket Ground
as he stood, shy and huge
  smiled, and wrote for me.
I loved him.

Then his friend Gilchrist came whirling
pounding, stamping, hurling
he bowled bullets at my countrymen.
This was sport, but something else too.
He moved with a fury
  an anger like a storm

like the Mau-Mau he was a soldier
like the men in Malaya he was a guerilla
like the warriors in Cyprus he was a hero
a new world was rising in the tornado of his arms
the trajectory of his hurling was at the heart of all things evil.

Then a man named Collie Smith
  swung his bat like a sword
he had a sword in his hand
and something new was sweeping England's turf
something heavier was rolling the ground
and cutting from the past.
When Wes bowled
magnificence was born for me
I never knew it before
I tried, I strove, I imitated
I found my own way,
  my own action
and every time I hurled
    I sought to touch his power.

Now I have lived in black lands of freedom
made common ground by systems of love,
the mist of history is clearing
and Balthazar's polish seems to take a new hue
and ground from the skin
  deep into my flesh and bone
the truth is forever growing -
Gilchrist's Caribbean is our common ground
the mountains of Ethiopia are our common ground
Ilford Cricket Ground is our common ground
the earth of tomorrow is our common ground.

What I Have Learned
To George Louison and Jacqueline Creft

I have learned
that work
transforms the world
  which is why I love
the workers of the world.

I have learned
that the skin is nothing
and what matters
   lies inside the skin
beyond the skin.

I have learned
     that knowledge
sets the human free
       but knowledge comes
through work and food
from production
and production comes
from our common earth
our common ground.

I have learned
     that freedom is not easy like a breath,
that we must build it
     carve it, shape it
make it :
    it is the antidote to death.

I have learned
    that humans are fuller
than their vastest dreams

   and that together with nature
there is nothing
       beyond their plan.

I have understood
that from this island
that out of the whips
       the blood and the shackles
out of the cutlass
the sweat and the struggles
out of revolt and the gall of the sugar
the howl of rebellion blasts across the world
and the hibiscus blossoms like flames
and the immortelles
       red as the blood of love
as the rippling circle
of people's power
throw out their awakening flower
over the aspiring earth.

Banner

The sea licks
on the slice of grey sand,
the Carenage burns in the sun
and schooners' masts stand like
warriors.

The Empire Cinema
        announces
Coming Attraction.
Under these words
someone has hung a banner.
It says
   Justice and Equality.

The sea breaks
Reagan shakes
Grenada makes
       freedom.

The White Man's Poem to the Black Man

To Maurice Bishop

'Not even skin deep !' I say
    is the difference
between you and I.
A lone, majestic star over the bay
    breaks the hole
in our sky
    of this night made dark between us
by the centuries of those systems' crimes
        that pain us.

Between us there is no mystery
  no guilt
no fear, nor recompense for times of torture -
we are not prisoners of history
    neither convicts of culture -
we *make* both
with our hands clasped fast together
when we scream out the binding words
      'Forward ever,
backward never !'

On this beach
the indiscriminate stones pile
left by the surge of the tide
    black, white, speckled
tossed and reconciled
each reflecting its pride
shining like freedom
from a common sun
the light, the strength,
  the truth of everyone !

'No more !' I say, black brother,
    can they order us
amongst you with rifles.
    'Never again !' I say
never another
    human life swapped for trifles.
Side by side
    the power is ours
the great divider
    Imperialism, cowers.

Why the problem ?
    Why the fuss ?
Nature, our comrade
built us thus -
we work with her
    as we must
to transform her flesh with one united kiss
of our hearts
    our skins
 our minds, our blood
we shall not sink back, drowning
    into history's flood !

No ! Like spangled butterflies
    our children crack the moment
testing their power, they rise
    into the future's ferment
side by side
    they find new flowers,
a world unfurled
    which is theirs and ours !

Windward Song

as dark as pearl
love streams like Zambesi
from the gift of night
island of paradox
strong as its hills
meandering coves
a history that wills
a resistance that loves
what feeling fills
your heaving heart
like waves with no end
and waves with no start
so little, so small,
is what I bring
in you there is all
it is of this I sing

Burston Fireplace

to heat the mind
to warm the flesh
to make the blood flow
    in the veins and arteries
of fifty striking children
    and their teachers
as defiant as life
as rebellious as brain
as the crackling coal fire
in the stone fireplace
in the Norfolk corner
of the classroom of the world
are three words
 real words
 key words
 teaching words
 learning words
 Burston words
 Soweto words
 Barbiana words
 Frelimo words
 Pitsmoor words
 Grenada words
 Stepney words
'freedom
      justice
            humanity'
words of your hearthstone
your heartstone
as Annie Higdon taught
she spoke these words
Tom roared them too
in this classroom as much as

union meeting rooms
to teach and organise in nothing
but the real world
the world of throbbing people
and their monuments
the true world of work
and in a world of classes
and a world beyond class
beyond race and clan
the foundation stones
    make up the walls
of labour and union
the whole school raised
on this effort and endeavour
while children learned
on these bare boards
while they skipped and played
on the molehilled green outside
and their teachers taught
and learned too, like them.
Hardly a hill here
flat fields and pastures
the height is the hedgerows
and the aspiring trees
anglian ditches and sodden green here
yet the mountains are in these words
the Andes Rockies Himalayas
Pennine to Kilimanjaro
'justice
    freedom
        humanity'
lighting their fires in the world
in a billion fireplaces

as they did in the minds of fifty striking children
as a dark world went to war
and their loving loyal parents
farmworkers and railwaymen
housewives and church tenants
marched on the brink of deadly trenches
my grandparents too
but those words of a fireplace
the basement of our teaching
the summit of our learning
the message and the answer
    of all our struggles
words to read
    words to speak
words to watch
    words to manifest
they'll do for us.

Her First Letter

She had received hundreds in her life
but the one which arrived today
in Ade Offa village
was truly her first letter.
It was the one that she could read
with this new power
given by her grandson, Neway.
The world splashes with meaning
across the dry earth
and life bursts like a spring
with new words
       on a sheet of paper.
On earlier days
  she took her daughter's lines
to a man at the other end of the village.
He could read
    one of the few, he was.
She paid him scarce money
to read out these close words to her,
and he would gossip
       over every threshold
and spill the messages meant for her alone.

Now her daughter's words are hers
her thoughts are hers
and her neighbours will know no more
than what she wants them to know !
Now she can read
now she can write
and what arrives for her
shall have her reply
and shall travel

      two provinces away
to make this one with her own flesh and love
in this revolution of knowing
      and expressing
this language of the mindful heart !

Sidamu, Ethiopia, 1989

Food of Words

He said
> lowering his well-thumbed book
> and looking to his crops, he said :

'These words are food
they made my family eat
they brought water to my fields
they helped me choose
> the healthiest seed

and throw away those that will not grow.
They showed me how
> to fertilise my land
> to bring water to my land

give nourishment to my life
give money to my pocket.
A clutch of words
a prize of food
all this I have read
and I have taken out words
and given back wheat
> to my children.'

Sidamu, Ethiopia, 1989

To Sylvia Under the Eucalyptus Trees

I had to look hard to find you
In the holes of sunlight
There under the eucalyptus leaves
Among the stones of the Ethiopian patriots.

I asked the man who kept the cathedral
Where you were lying.
And in our foreign words of Europe
I stumbled out your name
That I had known in the streets of Bow
In the dreadnought of our people's struggle.

Loving what you had done
In the life of two continents,
I read a poem of children over your bones
And saw the flesh of the future all around us -
As I watched them playing in their pathways
That lead from Africa
To the blocks of London.

Addis Ababa, 1989

Birdsong

Through the window of my classroom
at the very same level as my flipchart
two doves outside on a willow branch
sit between the flourishing leaves
shining with the season's showers,
and they stare at my pedagogy.
Maybe they are common pigeons
        I'm not sure
and I'm the last poet to be a birdwatcher
but this *is* a poem, I think,
        so let me call them doves !

On the next tree, a fir, in a fork of branches
another half-hidden sphere of feathers
        squats on a nest
and also looks through the window of the learning humans
past a small tree sprouting like a stranger
through the mortar of the border of our roof.

I talk about Spring with my students
about a season of hope, of watering, of bursting life
while a cherry blossom makes pink snow
letting loose its briefly-given petals
fluttering down as soft and transient loveleaves

Against the black galvanise of the steelworks
in Attercliffe's old world of endless rainclad grey
my student Elham sees the doves and their birdstare,
she talks new words about her family in Baghdad
and the forty-two of them dead like the desert.
She weeps for them, occupied and refettered,
while outside in the Sheffield air

floats dust which is not Iraqi dust
but dust which must be filtered just the same.

So what is this cloudy Spring for us, for all of us ?
Is it only to reconstitute our sorrows ?
Is it to break with the old oppressive ways
to learn a new language of hope and strength
to find new life from these old words ?

These old words of Shakespeare, Swift and Keats
these old words which Blake spun as a puzzle of blessing
these old words which these earnest birds hear
            through the kindling rain
these old words which burn every day
which give fire to our new world
and meanings and truth to expose the old
even amidst these vast, decrepit forges,
words which are Elham's now too
and all these learners from Sudan,
new wordsters from Yemen, from the Congo and Kabul -
our words ! Create with the people
    borrow this birdsong
    the imagination's sheen
    the Spring leaf's freshness
    the exploding blossom's colours
    the food of earth and shower
    the brilliance of this new season
    the brain and love of others
from this concrete classroom too, and tell well
the human's cosmic search for freedom
and the daily story
        of her endless finding.

Made

Old men, old men
  old Arabian men
in this house you bought together
decades ago in struggling years
still your centre
        still your hub
staggering up the stairs
        with your sticks
coming to learn English
        to talk, to joke
        to sing that
'This land was made
for you and me'
and sing Woody's words
with such foundry power
a Vulcan's fury of laughter
as the forgotten sticks
        stand in corners
        against shelves
        against radiators
lean against filing cabinets
shake with their own
        transmuted nature
and want to sing too
grow green again from Burngreave to Shaibi
old men, old men
you of the great hammers and rollers
shake on with your humour
your life made of steel
made in Sheffield
on a million knives and forks
like those I ate with every day
as a boy, as a boy

the hallmark clear and proud
stamped across you too
you and Woody's Okie song
made into Yemen
made into dustbowl
made into Yorkshire
made into the world.

Poem for Shaif

Old man on a stony Yorkshire hill,
Warm and friendly Arab of steel
Size belying the power of the mind
Now at the end of your journey
You look over your valley of a working life
Over demolished foundries, uprooted rolling mills
Furnaces doused by history, forever melted steel
After the miles through crag and sea and land
Through a canal reclaimed by brothers,
Arab with laughing, radiant eyes
Man of Yemen, elder of Sheffield
Two places of living, but one life
Two sets of hills but one mountain climbed
A colonial power repulsed, a partition repelled
A village from the rocks to a city of
          sleeting streets
From the stepped farm terraces to foreign
          factory gantries
A village to leave, a far community to build
A people to unite, a world to win.
You went some way, old man of Shaibi,
And those who leave and love you
will carry on your journey.

Adjectives

today brothers
we're going to learn about
    adjectives
    yes, *adjectives*
what is that, *Attercliffe* ?
I live and work there
    thirty years
all of we did that.
Not *Attercliffe* Kassim, *adjectives*
but what was it like there
in the steelworks, tell me now.
It was dirty
and hot man, hot like hell
  in the foundry
and the gaffers shouting all day
and up in the crane
no break all the shift
high up and dusty
and the noise man,.
the hammers in my ears
even now when I sleep
thunder, thunder
they wonder so many of us are deaf
and dangerous too
in the rolling mill
my friend from Shaib
a rod went through his leg
they took it off
and me too
I had the tongs
    with an English bloke
we had a burning bar

he say something to me
but I don't understand
he dropped his end
the bar fall on my foot
you see these hospital shoes
for forty years I have them
dangerous, man, dangerous.
Yes, *adjectives*.

My Two Grandmothers

I

essex girl
victorian girl
daughter of a squire
a fat farm's family
in green sinking pastures
september fields of wheat
and lands of easy wealth
essex girl
loved a poor man
a father's gamekeeper
a man of rabbits and hares
a class of woods and fences
essex girl
disinherited for love
essex girl
in Coggleshall and Kelvedon
six children in a small house now
the boys will work for squires
will tramp the fields and furrows
mind the pigs and cows
but the girls,
essex girls
victorian girls
go to the city
go to service
find a family
farewell to the fields
to the misty dawns
the damp of the night
to a London basement
or high attic room
to trays and brooms
teapots and china cups

dusters and brushes
made-in-Sheffield cutlery
pinafore girl
London girl
in that house of brick
in a Stoke Newington street
you became a new daughter
that house of Jews
took you as a daughter
house of love in London
the newspapers every morning
Mr Gladstone this
Mr Disraeli that
and the fields far away
the animals a dream
a dream of essex

I met you turning seventy
for twenty years I loved you
getting in your coal
addressing your envelopes
to my auntie Connie
to your daughter down under
a war bride from Romford
who married an anzac
after that war of wars
the loss of emigration
>   *4 Nicklin Streeet*
>   *Coorparoo*
>   *Brisbane*
>   *Queensland*
>   *Australia*
every week for all those years

and you never saw her again
and I never saw her once

you stay with me always
your tea and toast dripping
I sit in your chair
as I write those words
smoothed by your body
shining with your movement
rubbed by your life
wood of your history
you're in me still
your rebellion and love
your kindness and energy
essex girl

II

Alice from the place
that everyone sang about
how it was a long way to go
and a long, long way to come from

Alice comes to England
from across the Irish Sea
like millions like her
she marries a toymaker
a fervent conservative
and makes thirteen children
lives near Clapham Common
and dies

>   still a young woman
>   still a country girl

Alice what did you think
when your husband ranted
        for empire
when as a Tory councillor
he went to France in 1916
to stir up weary Tommies
across a channel of blood
to fight the Germans
and charge from their trenches
and die and become nothing
as their bodies became the earth
and their whiskey field marshal
laid a foundation for a statue
in royal Whitehall
and you loved thirteen children

And how did you feel
        really feel
as you played with your children
amongst the Easter eggs in 1916
when British soldiers
        cut down your people
when the guns ripped Dublin
when they strapped James Connolly
        to a chair
while his wounds bled freedom
and they tore up his holed body
        with their bullets

my mother
        your thirteenth
        was three then

she knew you for a few years
before you travelled on
        a long long way,
but Alice what did you think
while you were here, so fresh
what thoughts behind that brow
inside that human-bearing body
that helped to make me
who never knew you
who never felt the rays of your Irish eyes
I wonder as many times
        as they sang that song
across imagined years
made real by our histories

As My Mother Knits Blankets for Ethiopia

now arthritic fingers can knit no more
yet for years
        your needles clicked
in the dim sitting room light
while the television chuntered in the corner
you who never strayed from England
trapped in the suburbs
        of a privet compound
whose father was a conservative
so his daughters were conservatives
whose husband feared Africa
so his wife feared Africa -
have so much love inside you
        love I know
from the first steps
through all the migration of my life
love now given to Africa
        in surprise
to the unknown Ethiopian
        as you knit
piece after piece
        square after square
in wools of all the colours of the world
and then stitch together
into cosmic blankets
no shyness here for Africa
in the sitting room behind the hedges

yet so private is this humanity
so retired
so leashed in unknowing
but so strong in intuition

for people elsewhere
                need warmth
there in the equatorial eye
                of a searing sun
                need warmth
and make it for themselves
                and others

yours erupts from these suburbs
                inside these wallpapered rooms
beside the family photographs
the potted plants and Constable prints
of hayfields, ponds and oak trees
how much it yearns to spill
across the acres of a struggling earth
                and its faraway continents
how much of it stays contained
with father
                husband
                            children
and the power battering down love
                and consciousness
to the house
                only the house
and the children of the house
and the shops and iron and sink
and the duties of the stove
                to fill up everyday

now this knitting
                is not a liberation
it cannot be a shout for freedom
but it is a labour

    an old woman's love
a surprise of life for the human
    uncovered
        as a blanket
tossed by its corner
across a homely bed
as the body steps from sleep
and moves daywards
    to its morning tasks
with a caring energy
that still can change the world

Felixstowe, 1989

No Supertram Over Here !
Millhouses Cricket Club, 1860-2003

Carpenters and clerks, gardeners and teachers,
painters and taxi-drivers, steelmen and shopkeepers,
men dressed in a grubby white
playing in the stone shadow of a mill
under the roof of giant willows
next to the spin of a bowling brook
striking, diving, throwing, running
        deciding, working together,
marking a boundary, rolling a pitch of life -
this is a field of the company of common people
where old men watch from benches on the margins
where millions have walked and played in a park of joy
where children throw stones in a hurrying stream
where strolling lovers kiss to the clip of a bat
where men are suddenly boys again
as they splash and leap across Pennine water
from half-submerged stone to stone
to find their sodden ball, smashed by a rival.

1860 hard-hitting pioneers who knew the Chartists
twentieth century settlers from Sharrow and the Hallam hills
who marvelled at Rhodes and Bradman
from Bramall Lane's benches
millennium Sheffielders from Pakistan and the Caribbean
from all the world's suburbs of the sun
to where the Derbyshire clouds grey their way
up the long treeclad valley of the Sheaf
to break up the play with sudden angry showers

Who would cut away such a life of green?
Who would demolish the people's skills and pleasure
and face history with such contempt?

The hook of fury, the diving slips,
the angular spin, the bat's grace and power
the howling appeal, the mindful stratagem,
the careering stumps, the coruscating drive
all the excellence of the ordinary
all the play of our democracy,
hold on fast to your bat of dreams
hurl your ball to the centuries that come.

Third Man

standing at third man
under the loping willows
at dogshit corner
inside the boundary hedge
watching Danny
hurl them down
at the far end
and thinking
life's game goes on
playing it hard
as Azhar screams an appeal
searing
like the beep of his taxi
as the batsman
from the peak village
gripping his palate
pressing down on his handle
determined, dogged,
smiling inwardly
plays it humanly.
I watch the contest
waiting for the edge
I lurch among the curling leaves
like an old bird perching
taking breath for the chase
arching up the arms
for the throwback

Comrade Cricket I salute you
you bring me
a world which is local
you keep me human
you keep me social

one the bowler
two the batsman
and me the third man
among thirteen
standing, looking, waiting
as ready as I will ever be.

Raising a Sightscreen

it is the banner of our Saturdays
white stained brown and green
by the rusty butcher's hooks
and the piles of mowed grass
'made in Sheffield'
      is the steel frame -
as it swings up suddenly
it can take your arm off
bowling arm
      batting arm
right or left

we screw the wheels in the base
we lay out the canvas screen
      on the trodden patchy turf
fix it on the wild frame
      with the mangled hooks
and four of us swing it upwards
flying like a mainsail
      over the people's park
in line with the stumps
and the batsman's focussed eyes
it's our marker
      our proud flag
and as Steve or Shiraz
clear it with their hitting
and the ball soars over
      its tired fabric
it stretches in pride for us
flutters in the wind
      sucks in the sun
and a game becomes a world.

Priceless

our corpuscles forge
the words in our blood
long live life
these words drum like Blakey
        in our heart
pound like Roach
        through our brain
and make their meaning through
        every vein and spore

beneath the palette of our skins
our blood knows the meaning
as it ripples through our brain
its streams and brooks
tell us what is true
    what is real
    what is precious
like the lives of children
more than anything
the lives of children

so how did your blood
conceive of Beslan, human ?
how did it shoot down Hector Pieterson
and all his classmates
in the streets of Soweto ?
torture and kill
        the young Emmet Till
        in Money, Mississippi ?
carry off like coal
the wise Anne Frank
and kill her in Belsen ?
Belsen Beslan

how close they are
>   in sound and death
how much the same inferno
and Soweto and Nyazhonia
My Lai and Jenin
for all their proprietors
made the blood of meaning pour from life's arteries
until it was washed away
>   meaningless
down death's long conduit
long live death they shouted
ghouls all
>   inhumans all

yet Anne in her attic
staring out at the chestnut tree
that glinted through the glass
wrote to all of us
'I feel the suffering of millions'
and at Beslan
it was the first day
>   of the new school year
and Georgy, ten years old
brought flowers for his teacher
then squatted next to
>   a woman with a bomb
he did what he was told
and put his hands behind his head
for three endless days
was blasted by dynamite and human flesh
plucked shrapnel from his arm
and told a news man
'one terrorist had twenty
>   children that were killed

      over there in Chechnya
      and because of that
they came to kill us'
and 326 were slaughtered
      priceless humans
      half of them children
Georgy also felt the suffering
even of the assassins
who shot his classmates in the back
and made the blood
           of their beautiful brains
flow like a delta
      like a thousand rivulets
across the earth and concrete
of this Caucasian land

land of humans
of human heart and brain
now stopped in shame and pain
as *long live death*
fuses blood with venom
as Anne Hector Emmet Georgy
shout out their words
      their affirmations
their refusal to serve death
and make their long long walk
grabbing life itself
      from the ghouls
and in their unison
in their world of children
they shout in each other's ears
in all our ears
long live life.

Ambushed

Flashes of memory
that stick to me
    like my own red skin
    blotched and chapped
me in a cowboy suit
squeezing the trigger
    of a plastic pistol
    and cracks from a cap gun
    aimed at Indians
the Sioux of my mind
forced into my head
by years of Saturday morning pictures
and Romford Odeon's Hollywood screen
and the serial heroes
    the serial killers
and comics' bleeding colours
running like war-paint
of canvas-covered wagons west
chased by howling braves
barebacked riders of death
and me firing behind
what stories of a lied-to childhood
across an ocean of dreams
these tales that frame the mind
    linger like bloodstains
    in the consciousness
and still surprise us
ambush us even now
how this canvas keeps showing through
whatever they do
whatever they teach
whatever they write

to paint it over
whatever analysis of class
of race and class
that we formulate
the imperial murder
the blood of conquest glows through
seeps through
    into children's poems
the genocide bleeds into the present
and it still kills
suicide of youth
fetal alcohol syndrome
drugs aids the rez the bantustan
made in England
from continent to enclave
while the Empire takes the rest.

If we had known our history then
if they had but taught it
to us in our short grey trousers
and our short back and sides
and school caps and peaks pulled down
to cover our forbidden quiffs
our nascent brains
if they had told us this in our classrooms
as real knowledge
    the antidote to lies
to scissor through to the palimpsest
    with our young minds
to find the blood of the people
    in this, our same world
    red blood
    redskin blood

how would we have painted anew
to wash away the map of Empire
and its not-so-indelible red
across all our worlds
and paint the red of people .

So you children Mohawks all
as I read and mark your poems
as I struggle to know you and your history
in knowledge and in friendship
as a teacher must
after so much hate in earth and film
now the fire of your language
the arrows of your words
hit me in the head
in my heart.

Tyendinaga Mohawk Territory, Canada, 2005

Toronto Transit

nearly four decades past
escaping England
I first came here
a city on the edge
of the pristine
ocean-crossing families
generations displaced
    and recovering
the furies and wounds
    of wars healing
and their children building
but it was white as winter
    untouched unmixed
    unblemished white
except for its true proprietors
its first ravaged peoples
and those whose forebears
    arrived at the first and last station
    of the cruellest track

it was beautiful then too
    huge and without limits
    sublime after Europe
    after the nazis
    after a universe of war
an endless land of hope
disappearing to the north
besieged to the south
in land and lakes
in prairies and mountains
and Toronto on the cusp

but how much more beautiful now
even on this bus rolling
along Finch between Jane and Dufferin
and the world has come to stay
 not for a weekend
 but for time unleashed
and it sits on these seats
Ghana nestling on a Tamil shoulder
two of half a million Italians
    Greeks and Poles
    with all the Americas
Chile to Whitehorse
Panama to Yellowknife
and China shares the aisle
with the bats of Pakistan
with Trinidad's children
Bengali scarves
and the prams of Iran
and war's grand-orphans
make community together
and a thousand tongues speak
in this new city of cosmos.

York University, Toronto 2004

Passage

I want to see our words
put food in the mouths of children,
I want to see them
    digging the earth with forks
and pulling out cabbages, onions and yam.
I want to see our words
    vaccinating ill people
stopping their shuddering
    giving them health.
I want to see our words
    dismantling missiles
    disintegrating bombs
freeing my country from being
the first line of defence for imperialism.
I want to see our words
    growing like bluebells
    over the graves of hatred
I am tired of the words which bring sickness
sick of the Queen's English
and of Bush English. Blair English
I hate profiteering words
    for they rip up lives
I hate useless words
    for they hide what is true
    and they decorate deceit
I hate lying words
    because they kill people
I want our words to be solid
    like new houses for people
    when love enters with them
prosperous like growing maize stalks
    or an organised factory

          under workers' control
a spacious school
    throbbing with democracy
a simple red melody
    sung by millions
I want our words
to live as long as we do
        then they belong to others.

Hello Siva

'We are here because you were there.'
A. Sivanandan

Hello Siva
        I'm here again
because you were there.
Tamil boyo
        global insighter
        King's Cross joker
        human of cosmos
ideas through prisms of resistance
storms of life and beauty
agonies and joys of history
all around the alleyways of Gray's Inn Road --
here and there, race and class
        met in our brain
to make the now and future.
Open the batting of struggle!
First change of strategy!
        I'm there again
because you're here.

The Bridge
For Daniel and Russell

Walking through Sheffield station
crossing the bridge
                 a short cut for me.
Then coming towards me
a group of school children
                 seven, eight year olds
out of school and happy
dressed in plastic jackets
their school was written
                 all over them,
a life-name of learning
                 'Waterthorpe School'
and bubbling they were
                 marvelling at trains
running to look down
seeing and watching
to read their destinations
Leeds, Barnsley, Cleethorpes
and sense their movement,
their rumbling from the station.

Who could not be with them?
And my age plummets
    my memory quickens
the trains of my early morning
                 in the London suburbs
come steaming towards me
hurtling through the platforms
smoking coal giants
roaring beasts of boyhood
and I stopped still

transfixed by daydreams
until the last child passed
a girl of two races
                she smiled at me
her eyes flashed pathways
her flesh and blood shone
as a moment of forever
                she waved her hand
lifting it to a face of beauty
like a flag of the human future.

I came back to our morning
like an explorer come home
I left the past
                like a finished journey
I crossed the footbridge
           and went towards work
with her smile in my every cell
and saw a world of hope to walk in.

Notes

A Dream of Alfred Linnell
Alfred Linnell was an unemployed worker from the East End of London. He was killed in November 1887 when mounted police assaulted an unemployment demonstration.

Strike of Words
On 28 May 1971 the children of Sir John Cass and Redcoat Secondary School, Stepney, went on strike in solidarity with the author, who had been sacked for publishing their poems in the community anthology *Stepney Words*.

Poem for Blair Peach
Blair Peach was a young New Zealand teacher killed on an anti-fascist demonstration in Southall, London in 1979.

Des Warren's Eyes
Des Warren was one of the pickets gaoled at Shrewsbury following the national building workers' strike of 1972.

Victor Jara
Victor Jara was a Chilean folk-singer and a Communist, who was murdered during the US-backed military coup in Chile in 1973.

Plant the Tree of Freedom Everywhere !
The title is taken from a speech made in 1978 by Samora Machel, President of Mozambique.

George Lansbury's Dream of Poplar
George Lansbury (1859-1940) was the leader of Poplar Labour Council in 1921 when its councillors were gaoled for refusing to raise the local council rate.

Hawksmoor's Lantern
Nicholas Hawksmoor (1661-1736) designed many London churches, including St Anne's, Limehouse.

Island Winds
Arnaldo Tamayo Mendez was a Cuban cosmonaut and the first black man in space.

Beloved Banditti
The Anglican Church of St George's, Grenada, contains a marble plaque listing the names of the 'Proprietors and inhabitants of this colony' who died during the Fedon rebellion of 1795 at the hands of 'an execrable Banditti', who 'stimulated by the insidious arts of French Republicans / Lost all sense of duty to their sovereign / And unmindful of advantages they had long enjoy'd, / By participating in the blessings of the / BRITISH CONSTITUTION.'

Maurice and Samora at Seamoon
In 1982 President Samora Machel of Mozambique and Maurice Bishop, Prime Minister of Grenada, spoke at the Africa Liberation Day rally at the Seamoon Stadium in Grenada. 'Kannimambo' is a Mozambican song, meaning 'thank you'. 'Forward March' was the anthem of the Grenada revolution.

To the Cuban Doctors of Grenada
Che Guevara and Agostinho Neto (the first President of the People's Republic of Angola) originally trained as a doctors ; Norman Bethune was a Canadian doctor who served with the Chinese revolution, later in Spain; Cheddi Jagan was the elected leader of Guyana whose government was suppressed by the British in 1953; he was originally a dentist. Frantz Fanon was a trained psychologist, active in the Algerian war of independence.

A Sloop called *Success*
Success is the name of a small sloop which used to carry the mail, cargo and passengers between Grenada and Carriacou.

Balthazar's Poem
Wesley Hall, Collie Smith and Roy Gilchrist were all members of the West Indies cricket team which toured England in 1957.

Burston Fireplace
The School Strike in Burston, Norfolk, began in August 1914 when the teachers in the village school, Tom and Annie Higdon were dismissed. Parents and students built an alternative 'Strike School' in 1917, which remained open until 1939.

To Sylvia Under the Eucalyptus Tree
The pioneer revolutionary and feminist Sylvia Pankhurst spent the last years of her life in Ethiopia. She is buried in a eucalyptus grove in Addis Ababa.